Benny and Willy with the Three Bean Machine. Uxbridge, ON. 2015.

BE A FOOL

BAD ART CLUBS, TALL BIKES, AND A DIY PHILOSOPHY FOR CREATIVE OUTSIDERS

A VISUAL MEMOIR BY THE ZENGA BROS.

Written by Willy Zenga & Benny Zenga

Nine Ten Publications Inc.
Vancouver
ninetenpublications.ca

Library and Archives Canada Cataloguing in Publication

Title: Be a fool : bad art clubs, tall bikes, and a DIY philosophy for creative outsiders : a visual memoir by the Zenga Bros. / written by Willy Zenga & Benny Zenga.
Names: Zenga, Willy, author. | Zenga, Benny, author.
Identifiers: Canadiana (print) 20260230251 | Canadiana (ebook) 20260230286 | ISBN 9781738360789 (softcover) | ISBN 9781738360796 (PDF)
Subjects: LCSH: Zenga, Willy. | LCSH: Zenga, Benny. | LCSH: Creation (Literary, artistic, etc.) | LCSH: Creative ability. | LCSH: Art—Philosophy.
Classification: LCC N70 .Z46 2026 | DDC 700.1—dc23

ISBN (print): 9781738360789
ISBN (ebook): 9781738360796

Editing by Kim Werker
Copyediting by Michelle Woodvine
Proofreading by Kim Werker
Book and Cover Design by Willy Zenga and Benny Zenga
Cover Photo by David Zenga

AI was not used in the writing, editing, or design of this book.

Production of this book was made possible by the enthusiasm and financial support of readers, Zenga Bros. fans, and makers who backed the project on Kickstarter. Without you, dearest backers, this book would not exist. Thank you!

Visit ninetenpublications.ca for more books and zines about how to make things, how things are made, and why it matters. Made in Canada for creative people around the world.

Printed in Canada on Sustana Opaque™ SS FSC 80 lb 376ppi White paper, which is elemental chlorine-free and contains Sustana's 30% recycled fiber.

30% ECF PERMANENT

TREE TALL
KATANA
AIRPLANE MODE
HIGH HORSE
• Slim, lighter build
• Folding or removable racks
• Netting for duffel bag
• Big shot handlebars
• Rigging spots
• Tent bike
• Can also become sail
• Mounting points
• Split frame for transport
METALWORK
DADDY LONGLEGS
○ KUSTOM DETAILS
○ FLAME THROWER
○ MULTI BRAKE mount 20-29
WOODWORK
MOMMY LONGLEGS
○ WOOD RACK
○ PLYWOOD CLAMP ARM
CAMERA
MATATU
SPUTNIK
○ RUNNING BOARDS
This looks Rad
WILD DRAGSTER MODEL
WHAT'S AVAILABLE IN ZANY HANDLEBARS
TALL HORSE MEASUREMENTS
70"
34"
57"
TALL BIKE TREE FORT

Stephen and David test the structural integrity of the double-decker tall bike for the first time. Mission, BC. 2015.

CONTENTS

INTRODUCTION

This story begins at the dawn of the new millennium with my brother Benny and me, who, alongside our large eccentric family, set out to start an arts collective in our tired little town. At that time, we wanted to encourage local youth to tap into Wild Creativity. In undertaking this mission, on one fateful night, a mysterious philosophy was revealed to us: The Wisdom of the Three Beans: Create Everywhere, Redeem Everything, Be a Fool.

This book documents our journey as we've aspired to live by the Wisdom of the Three Beans. We could never have imagined that so many years later, we would still be plumbing the depths of what originally seemed to us a simple creative manifesto. This philosophy has radically impacted every area of our lives and has influenced the many projects and adventures chronicled within these pages.

This book tells the story of our unusual childhood and this mysterious philosophy that sparked a creative revolution in our lives. Since then, we've gone on to start a unique and influential arts collective, becoming groundbreaking designers and builders of adventure tall bikes, riding these radical creations in some of the most inhospitable environments in the world. We've produced award-winning films, and worked with legends in the worlds of skateboarding, snowboarding, surfing and BMX. We continue to build fantastic skateboard ramps and environments as well as public spaces and sculpture.

We believe the Wisdom of the Three Beans can positively transform the world. We've seen it in our own lives, yet in many ways, it's also made our lives infinitely more challenging. It put us on a road with no map to build a world with no instruction manual.

Wherever this philosophy came from, it has led us on a journey of creative expression that has been extremely rewarding and life-affirming.

Benny unloads all the pieces for the Belcarra High Up Hut from his tall bike onto the beach before rowing them out to the build site. Belcarra, BC. 2016. Photo by David Zenga.

THE REVOLUTION IS LIVING. BEGINNING AT THE
TURN OF THIS NEW CENTURY ~~THROUGH~~ ~~BROTHERS~~
A VISION WAS GIVEN ~~TO TWO~~ BROTHERS. TWO BROTHERS
OUT OF A FAMILY OF 11 ~~RURAL~~ SOUTH ~~LIVING~~
~~ONTARIO~~

STUNT BIKERS,
LY. A FAMI… VW
TOS ARTISTS … FAMILY
VISTS, RESTOR… FOODING WAS
WHERE…
ENCOURAG…
FIRST A… N
… PHILOSOPHY
THE… BEANS.

CREATE EVERYWHERE REDEEM EVERYTHI…
BE A FOOL.

~~…~~ TW3B THROUGH LIVING

THE WISDOM OF THE THREE BEANS

Our first meeting was at a condemned house on the outskirts of nowhere.

We gathered around a couple of beat up tables in the dingy basement of the tiny, one bedroom farmhouse under some hastily hung Christmas lights. Before us lay everything from mistint paint to paint brushes, glue, a few boxes of discarded toys, old dolls, and assorted recycled materials for our friends and some brave local teens to experiment with.

"This is a bad art club," we said. Criticism had no place there, and mistakes were met with laughter. Freed from the constraints of meaningless phrases like "good art," "fitting in," and the "real world," our Wild Creativity was set free. Bold experimentation was the process. The product was largely forgettable. Kids were painting all over their clothes, the walls, and the ceilings. A couple of mad scientists brought a punk rock franken-doll to life, and everyone generally made a huge mess.

By the time we all emerged from the basement into the cool night air, we knew that everything had changed.

Above: Claire DeAth and friend putting TVs to good use at an early Winking Circle meeting. Uxbridge, ON. 2001.

Opposite page: Benny and Willy back in the basement, contemplating the mysteries of the Wisdom of the Three Beans. Uxbridge, ON. 2017.

After everyone had left for the night, it was just Benny and me left standing under the stars behind the old house, emboldened and energized by what had happened at that first meeting. We had started the group inspired by DIY zines and books on outsider art and visionary environments. Our goal was simple: encourage local teens to be more creative in the face of the apathetic youth culture common to rural, middle-class towns like ours. After the excitement of that first meeting, we knew we were onto something.

We had all kinds of ideas for what the group could become, and we began to search for a core philosophy, a manifesto. Something that would be clear and memorable.

After struggling with this dilemma for a few weeks, we were getting frustrated. Then, one night when the two of us were together in the old farmhouse, something happened that Benny and I have talked about for years since, trying to make sense of how it really occurred. To this day, I can visualize the room perfectly in my mind—the maroon 1950s-style couch, the colorful oversized sitting cushions, papers, markers, and pens strewn across the worn Persian rug—but I can't remember the exact process we went through to come up with it.

The philosophy that became the guiding star for the collective and transformed our lives just seemed to materialize, fully formed, before us.

Seven simple words and one wonky symbol.

There it was. Three interlocking beans in a circle, drawn, as if by an unseen hand, on the sheet of paper between us. Each bean containing a cryptic phrase:

Create Everywhere. Redeem Everything. Be a Fool.

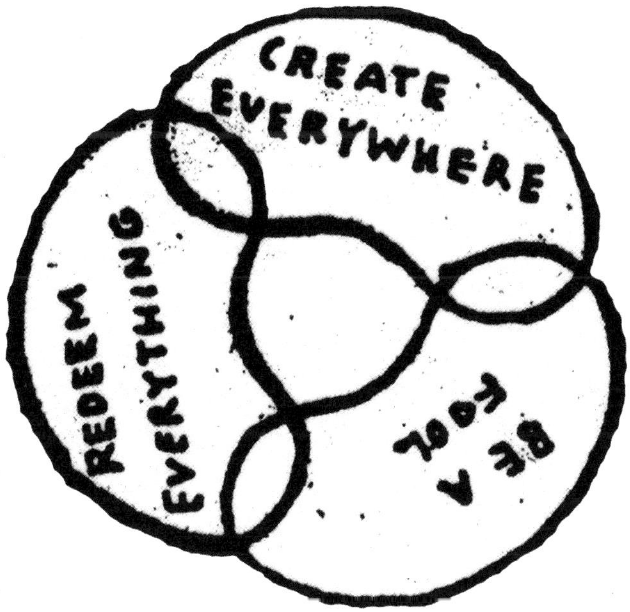

15

We sat contemplating it silently. It seemed to have just appeared out of nowhere. We don't remember editing it at all or working on any other possible phrases or designs. This was odd because, for so many of our projects, we usually went back and forth for hours, if not days, brainstorming and refining before coming up with an idea we liked.

Over the years we have wondered if there was a more palatable way to communicate to the masses our belief in the power of Wild Creativity that the Wisdom of the Three Beans revealed to us. But we always came back to the philosophy and symbol that was revealed to us that night. And since that night our understanding of its depth just continues to grow.

We have come to see that the Wisdom of the Three Beans is the Way of Infinite Creativity.

When we are on the Way of Infinite Creativity, we are connected to the Source, the Infinite, the Creator. We realize that there is no intermediary, no tool, technology, or device needed. We constantly express our innate—or wild—creativity. Throughout the book we move between the terms Infinite Creativity and Wild Creativity, as we understand these terms to be interchangeable.

The Way of Infinite Creativity is a path made up of nine steps. Three principles, three practices, and three purposes. These are more like dance steps that allow you to move through life in the most creative way possible, as opposed to steps that take you from the start to the end of a journey. The Way of Infinite Creativity is a journey that goes on forever and a beautiful dance that never ends.

Three Principles:
Create Everywhere / Redeem Everything / Be a Fool

Three Practices:
Make With Your Hands / Work With What You Have / Experiment Boldly

Three Purposes:
Build Dream Worlds / Transform Everyday Life / Express Reckless Optimism

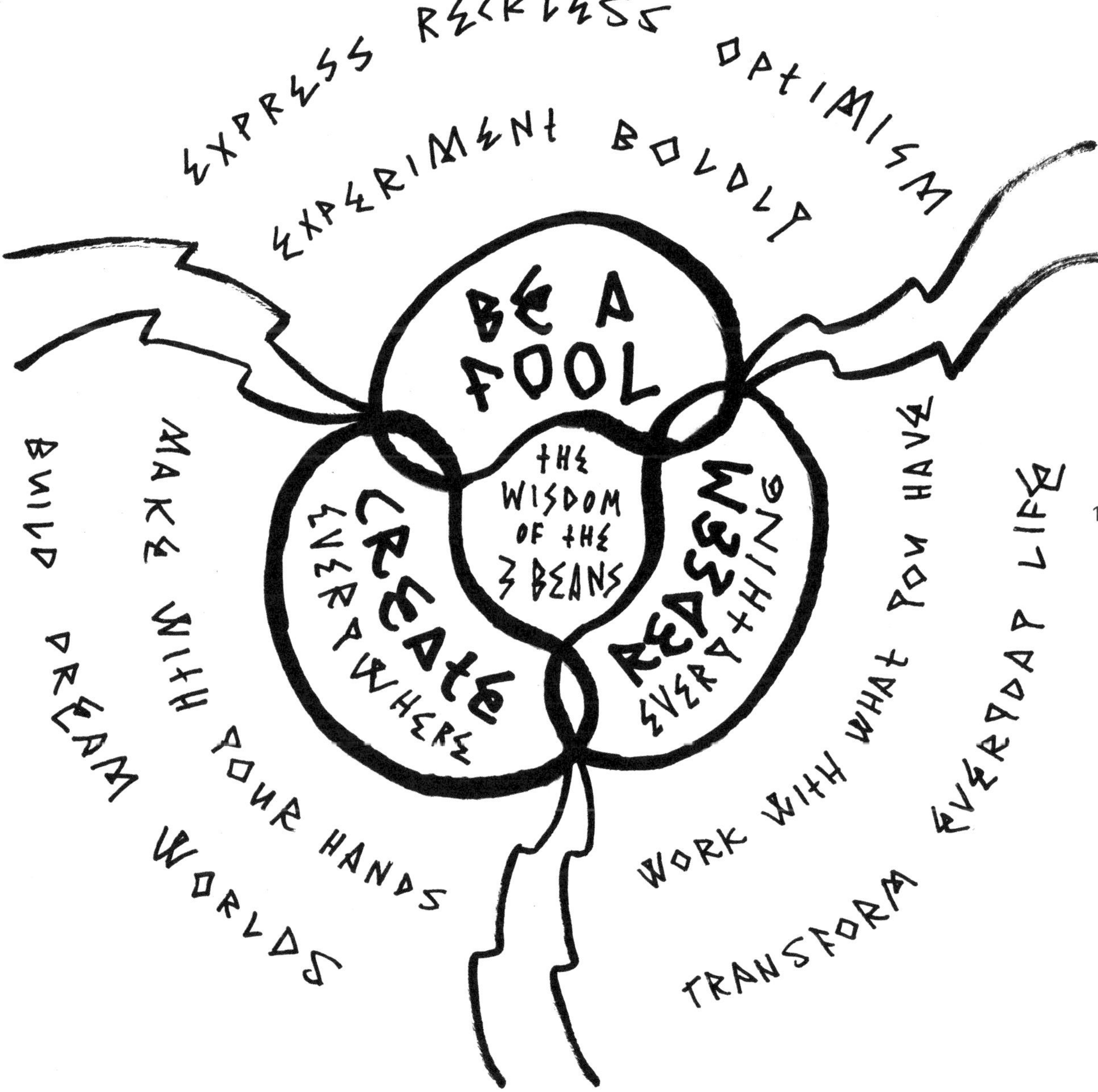
EXPRESS RECKLESS OPTIMISM
EXPERIMENT BOLDLY
BE A FOOL
THE WISDOM OF THE 3 BEANS
CREATE EVERYWHERE
REDEEM EVERYTHING
MAKE WITH YOUR HANDS
BUILD DREAM WORLDS
WORK WITH WHAT YOU HAVE
TRANSFORM EVERYDAY LIFE

THE WISDOM OF THE THREE BEANS

CREATE EVERYWHERE

MAKE WITH YOUR HANDS

BUILD DREAM WORLDS

REDEEM EVERYTHING

WORK WITH WHAT YOU HAVE

TRANSFORM EVERYDAY LIFE

BE A FOOL

EXPERIMENT BOLDLY

EXPRESS RECKLESS OPTIMISM

THE WAY OF INFINITE CREATIVITY

CREATE

EVERYWHERE

The Way of Infinite Creativity begins by making creation a constant practice. Seeing yourself as a creator is the foundational truth upon which everything else is built. This is a confirmation of who we are as human beings—a reclaiming of our true nature. You are alive, so you Create Everywhere.

No matter what you've been told or have come to believe, you are a creator, and within you is the Infinite. While it's easy to feel that your connection to the Infinite has faded through distraction and neglect, it will never go out. With renewed attention and by following the Wisdom of the Three Beans, the Infinite Creativity within you will begin to burn brightly once again.

To Create Everywhere means seeing yourself as a creative force—a maker, a builder—not just a spectator. It's about actively working to make things happen, rather than passively waiting for things to change. It is about bringing your ideas to life with your own two hands. Every aspect of your life can be touched by your creative impulse—your appearance, your possessions, your vehicles, and your home.

Above: Benny secures all the pieces of a High Up Hut onto his touring tall bike for the 40 km ride from Vancouver to Belcarra, British Columbia. 2016.

Opposite page: Belcarra High Up Hut install. 2016.

Previous spread: Benny enjoys the view from the completed Balcarra High Up Hut. 2016. All photos by David Zenga.

Each human being must recognize themself as a creator and an artist because that is what we are at our core. It is our birthright as human beings to contribute to the stories and songs, the art and architecture, the inventions, ideas and visions that make our human existence unfathomably rich and meaningful.

The goal is to move from the mindset of a spectator to that of a creator. We don't wait for someone else to make the world around us better: by the way we live each day, we are creating the world we want to live in.

10
BLNB 948

FOLK STUNTS

We can't explain why. Why were we drawn to the outsider, to the Holy Fool, to Wild Creativity? Why was fitting in not only unimportant but unacceptable? Why, instead of apathy, did we choose action? Could it have been our weird family?

Above: Benny circa 1982.

Right: Benny and Matt Ottenhof sandpit jumping. Uxbridge, ON. 1998.

Previous spread: Zenga Family caravan after crossing the border into the US during the Eccentrification Tour. Would you let these guys into your country? Blaine, Washington. 2011.

Christian jumps his 16" BMX bike over cardboard boxes during one of our many "Super Sunday Sessions" which gathered all the neighbourhood BMXers for jump ramp jams in our yard. Sandford, ON. 1999.

Legend goes that before my mom had any of us, she had said that she wanted seven boys. That legend was started by my mom herself, and after she gave birth to me (Willy) in 1972 she got busy fulfilling her prophecy. After me came Josh, then Benny, Aaron, Dan, Christian, and then Stephen. But she wasn't done yet. She decided that she wanted a daughter after all, so then came Robyn. And to the surprise of everyone, one more boy for good measure—David. Having nine kids was definitely uncommon, even back then, but what made our family more than a little unusual bordering on "weird," was the way my mom and dad ran their home.

It was always a house full of energy and action, with our parents encouraging each of us to express our own interests and passions. My creative journey started with drawing my own comic books, designing my own ninja weapons and costumes. Then came BMX and my dad building a backyard track for me. After that, skateboarding became the obsession. Zines were xeroxed, sweepers and layback grinds were filmed on VHS, and rickety quarter pipes were built from whatever material could be scavenged.

Super 8 frames from "Ski Boys," directed by Benny Zenga. 2006.

From top to bottom: Christian rides the road ski. Christian in a blue metal-flake helmet. Owen and David ride a toboggan outfitted with roller skate wheels. David, with a Super 8 camera attached to his handlebars, looks back at Benny through a hollowed-out TV.

With "Ski Boys," we decided to imagine ourselves as inventive teenagers, from an era decades before ours, before skateboarding, before "extreme", before action sports had been defined and commercialized.

Just some friends doing folk stunts—and getting rad-on whatever contraptions they came up with that afternoon.

Opposite page: Benny pond jumping. Uxbridge, ON. 1998.

My mom didn't worry about having a perfectly clean house or about kids going on the roof or setting up mattresses outside to jump on, or ramps in the front yard or in the driveway, or taking over the driveway with projects. Both of them just encouraged us to follow our own passions. They valued Wild Creativity over organized sports, and they still do to this day.

Because of this, our interests and adventures were as varied as the lengths of the bowl cuts we all sported. Whether through music or art, filmmaking or travelling, building ramps or skateboarding, we pushed each other to create and explore. Every day was a new adventure. We ventured across the farmland and into the forests surrounding us. We climbed cell phone towers, jumped off cliffs, and slept in abandoned barns.

We each developed our own unique set of passions and skills. I am a lifelong skateboarder, illustrator and writer. Josh is a mechanic, builder and engineer. Benny is a filmmaker, designer and builder. Aaron is a fabricator, photographer and writer. Dan is a musician and songwriter. Christian can do everything. Stephen is a mechanic and dabbler in fabrication, blacksmithing, and leatherwork. Robyn plays violin and piano, sings, and is a thespian—every family has at least one. David is a photographer and videographer. We're a pretty good mix of artists, builders, mechanics and engineers.

Top spread: Eccentrification Tour family portrait (left to right): Holly, Dad, Ellea, Mae, Will, Christian, Jordan, Owen, Aaron, Benny, Stephen, David, Mom, Dan, Jantina, Dawna, Robyn. Vancouver, BC. 2011.

Bottom row (left to right): Willy in his handmade ninja outfit. Benny in front of dads motorcycle. Mom in front of Dad's VW Beetle and Mom and Dad during their dating days. A typical breakfast with Dad as a young father.

MAKE WITH YOUR HANDS

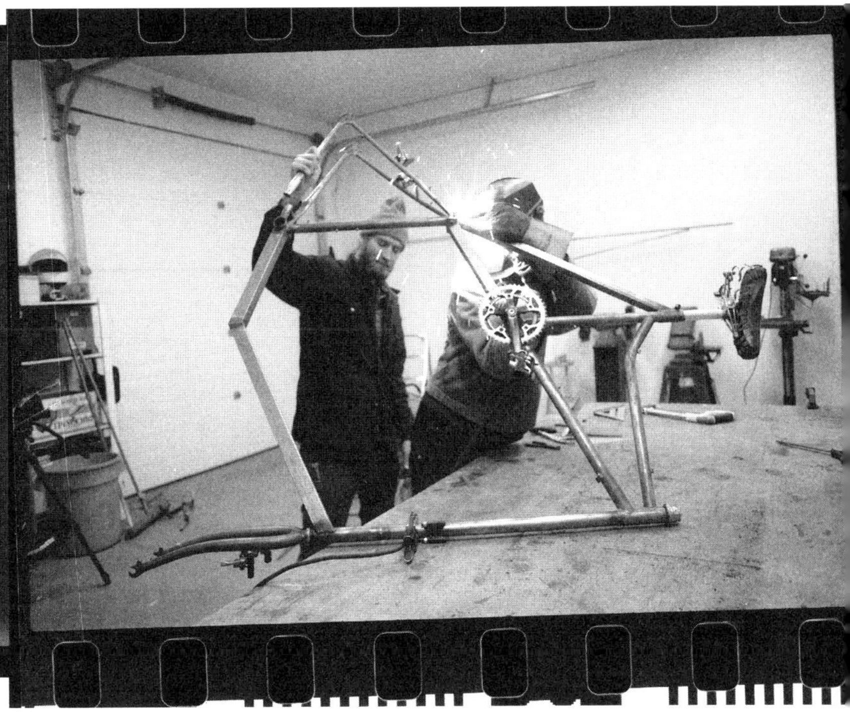

Above: Benny sliding a marker across paper wondering what will appear before him. Vancouver, BC. 2013.

Right: Aaron welds as Benny holds things in place during the building of an experimental tall bike frame. Aldergrove, BC. 2017.

To connect with your Wild Creativity, it is imperative that you start by doing. Tap into your innate creative source through action. Dreaming, scheming and planning will come later.

Start now. Move. Get your hands dirty. Be inside the question.

Through doing, making, exploring, and proceeding with wonder, answers and deeper questions are discovered. Action ignites creativity, builds motivation, and opens you up to serendipitous moments. Don't wait for inspiration.

In this day and age it is important for you to make things with your own two hands. Learn how to use tools so that you can build, make, and customize things yourself. The goal is to transform the physical landscape around you, and this cannot be done on your laptop or on your phone. As the digital realm increasingly invades every aspect of your life, it is imperative to learn to work with your hands to transform physical spaces.

Make something with your hands every day. Pause. Look down at your own hands and recognize the potential they hold. And recognize, too, how that potential is thwarted when there's a phone in your hands.

Autoplay is the death of inspiration.

Opposite page: A custom top tube badge for the Joy Machine, crafted by Christian Zenga at master goldsmith Ryan Corvus's studio in Vancouver, BC. 2012.

Below: Emily Zenga preparing for an art workshop at Two Rivers Gallery. Prince George, BC. 2018.

MAKE WITH YOUR HANDS

After you've shifted your paradigm—you see yourself as a creator, you're filled with wonder, you're seeing the world in a new way, you've faced fear and you're willing to try new things—now we start building this new world with our hands. Physically. That could be making your own clothes. Making meals from scratch instead of buying fast food or eating out all the time. Fixing things. Making things last. Working with your hands to build the physical world around you.

Action creates inspiration.

High Up Hut install at the Two Rivers Gallery. Prince George, BC. 2018.

TOOLS NOT TOYS

Our dad's philosophy was tools, not toys. So we had a garage full of tools and we were welcome to use any tools that we wanted—hammers, wrenches, power tools, saws, drills. We had many tools available to us that most kids our age would not be allowed to play with. Fortunately, we are still a family with eighty-eight fingers and twenty-two thumbs.

Skateboarding and BMX were threads that ran through our lives. Building our own ramps, trails, and dirt jumps was always central to that experience, from piling dirt over a stack of firewood to building quarter pipes, spine ramps, box jumps, half pipes, and kickers. In the winter, we filled abandoned barns with ramps. As soon as the snow thawed, we began digging and moving tons of dirt, shovel by shovel, wheelbarrow by wheelbarrow, transforming a vacant lot into a dirt jumper's paradise. When the rain fell, we rejoiced because it turned our dirt into gold, allowing us to form perfectly sculpted jumps. We never used the excuse that there was nothing around to ride. We built stuff to ride.

A few of us became gearheads, buying vintage Volkswagen vans and Beetles, restoring them, and spending countless hours on the side of the road fixing them. Along with the cars and vans, a love of old motorcycles was passed down from our father. From jumping dirt bikes to cross-continental road trips, old motorbikes were ridden hard, restored, rebuilt, and customized.

Previous spread: Stephen, Mom, Dad and Aaron in the garage as some old bikes get prepped for a new adventure. Mission, BC. 2013.

Opposite page (clockwise from top): Sandford dirt jumps. Sandford, ON. 2000. Willy with his tricked-out BMX. Markham, ON. 1984. Tsunami Ramp build. Uxbridge, ON. 2002. Willy with his Rat Fink board, handpainted by Christian. Uxbridge, ON. 2002.

Above: Stephen in his happy place. Vancouver, BC. 2011.

BUILD DREAM WORLDS

As we begin to transform ourselves, our stuff, and our spaces with our own two hands, we need to develop a vision of where we want to go and the kind of world we want to create. Consumer culture force-feeds us dreams crafted by marketers, but we must cook up our own visions. Is the dream of the world you want to live in truly your own, or is it one that was sold to you?

When you begin to see yourself as a creator, even the simplest actions can be done with love and grace. Whether it's making your bed in the morning, mindfully preparing breakfast, building something with your kids, or fostering community by connecting with friends in the evening, every action becomes meaningful. Instead of waiting for someone else to improve the world around you, you build your dream world through the way you live each day.

Take some time to imagine how your space can be a physical manifestation of your truest self. The goal is to change the world, so start with your own home. Make it into a place that makes people smile when they walk by. As you build the courage to customize and decorate boldly, your neighbours will begin to do the same, and soon you will have a street that celebrates individuality, joy and community.

When you are asleep you cannot dream another person's dream. When you're awake, make sure the dream you are working toward is your own.

Opposite page: Christian, getting ready to install his "Graffiti Living" project at Emily Carr University, Vancouver, BC. 2015.

Following spread: "Graffiti Living" design, build, and installation by Christian. Emily Carr University, Vancouver, BC. 2015.

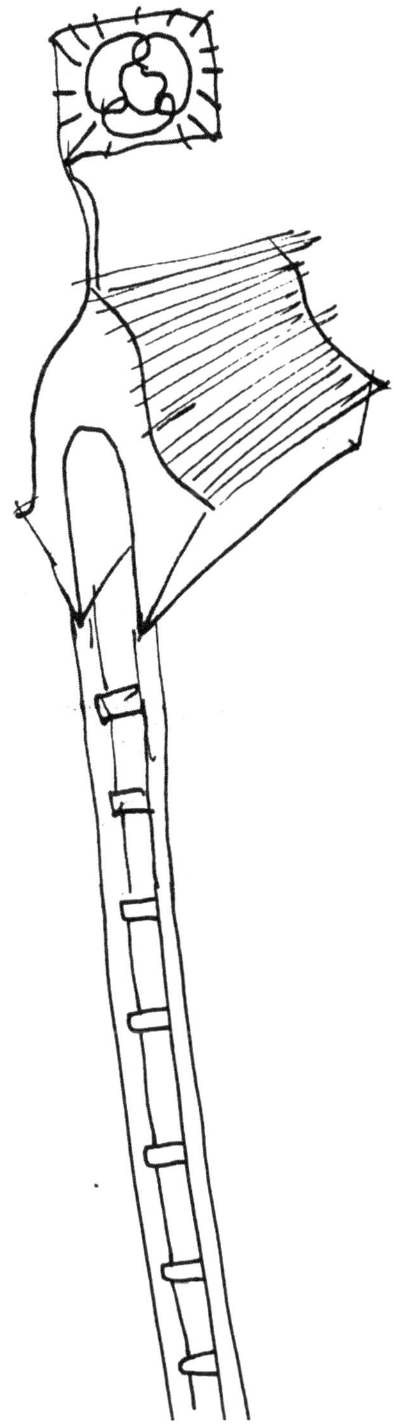

50

BARN RAMPS

We were BMX trail riders and we loved jumps. In the summertime we built dirt jumps that covered an entire acre of a vacant lot just down the road from our subdivision. But winters in Ontario are cold and long, and everything could be covered in snow from November to March.

So, during my high school years, and fuelled by our desperation to ride in the winter, we built a semi-secret skatepark in an abandoned barn on the outskirts of our small rural town. There were a few of these properties around town—with overgrown driveways, abandoned houses, full-sized, turn-of-the-century wooden barns with haylofts above and livestock areas below, old empty drive sheds, a rusted-out threshing machine in a tangle of long grass, just taunting you to climb it and remind you why you got that tetanus shot.

Previous spread: 6th Concession barn ramp. Uxbridge, ON. 1999.

Above: Dan flowing through the Sandford Trails on any given Sunday. Sandford, ON. 1998.

Right: Perfectly janky drop-in to box ramp in the 6th Concession barn. Uxbridge, ON. 1999.

The barn ramps were our winter solution, built by myself (Benny) along with my brothers Aaron and Dan and a few close friends who were willing to put in the hard work of building ramps for months in order to enjoy riding them for a few, precious hours at a time.

We collected all the scrap lumber we could and brought it out to the barn, hauling scraps of plywood and two-by-fours across snow-covered fields in the winter, and built a series of box jumps, quarter pipes, a vert wall...until we completely filled the barn with ramps.

We salvaged most of the wood from the abandoned farm house on the property. For months we steadily gutted it, carefully stripping out nearly all of its plywood and two-by-fours. We were doing a good deed by putting this old material to use rather than letting it rot into the ground or meet its inevitable demise when the developers would finally move in and flatten it to rubble in an afternoon. (We had watched this happen again and again in and around our small town: the steady spread of subdivisions replacing the charming old farm houses. It was painful knowing the beauty that those haunted-looking houses contained—gorgeous banisters and solid oak mouldings—was being crushed under bulldozer treads).

The Rail Ramp. Built for the Skate Heads video. Featuring Andy Anderson (layback grind) and Adam Hopkins (frontside air). Vancouver, BC. 2014. All images by Gordon Nicholas.

The Lagoon Ramp. Built for Swatch Nines at Waco Surf. Madars Apse (skateboarder) and Tya Zebrowski (surfer). Waco, TX. 2024.
Above photo by Theo Acworth. Opposite photo by Jorge Rivera.

swatch

MAKE WITH YOUR HANDS AS YOU BUILD DREAM WORLDS

This page: Dan and friends sculpting dirt jumps at the Sandford Trails. 1998.

Opposite: Illustration by Christian Zenga. 2024.

Christian and Benny repair the Beard Ramp. 2014. Photos by Gordon Nicholas.

Opposite page: Benny and Christian High Up Hut location hunting. Stave Lake, BC. 2014. Photo by Stephen Zenga.

REDEEM EVERYTHING

When you are on the Way of Infinite Creativity you Redeem Everything. You move from the mindset of a consumer to that of a redeemer. You look for ways to heal the brokenness of the world around you.

To Redeem Everything is to take that which has been discarded and turn it into something spectacular. To transform the practical into something magical.

As the insatiable desire for "new and improved" products fills landfills with millions of tons of trash, we instead look for ways to treasure what we already have and enjoy the challenge of finding what has been thrown away, forgotten, or rejected and transform it into something new and beautiful.

From a beat-up bicycle to a broken relationship, everything can be redeemed. Nothing is without hope or possibility and no one is beyond redemption.

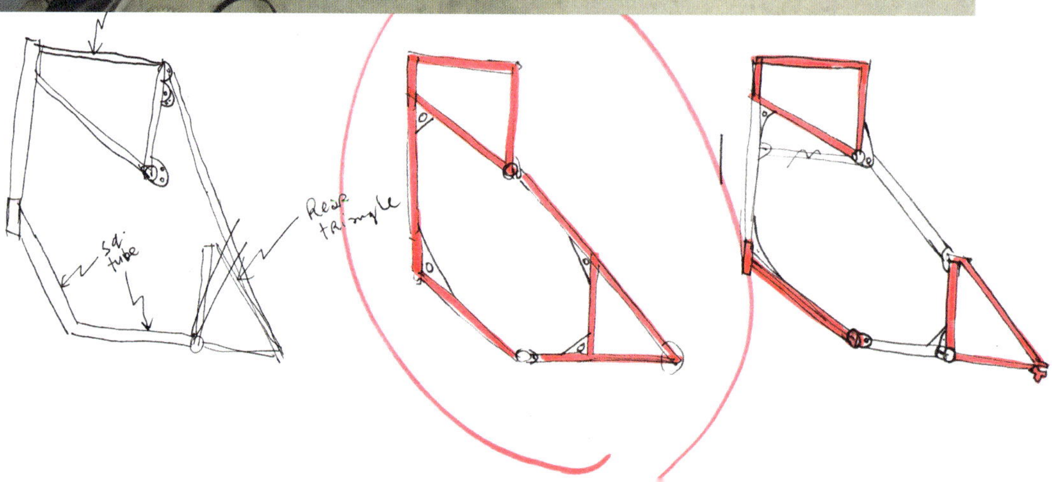

Above: David with the Swing Set Bike. High Park, Toronto, ON. 2015.

This bike was built out of a scrap swing set and discarded bike frames. The sissy bar is mounted on a Wee Willi Winkels skateboard truck, and most joints are just bolted together. It constantly sways back and forth as you ride, giving all but the most seasoned riders a serious bout of motion sickness. It's everything a performance bicycle shouldn't be, but it's so dang fun to ride. It's perfectly weird.

Opposite page: David consults the sacred geometry of the "Tree Tall" touring tall bike frame. Aldergrove, BC. 2017.

24147

Opposite page: Nate Lacoste is smooth. Here he combs back the Beard Ramp's hair with a nose bonk. Vancouver, BC. 2014. Photo by Graham Nicholas.

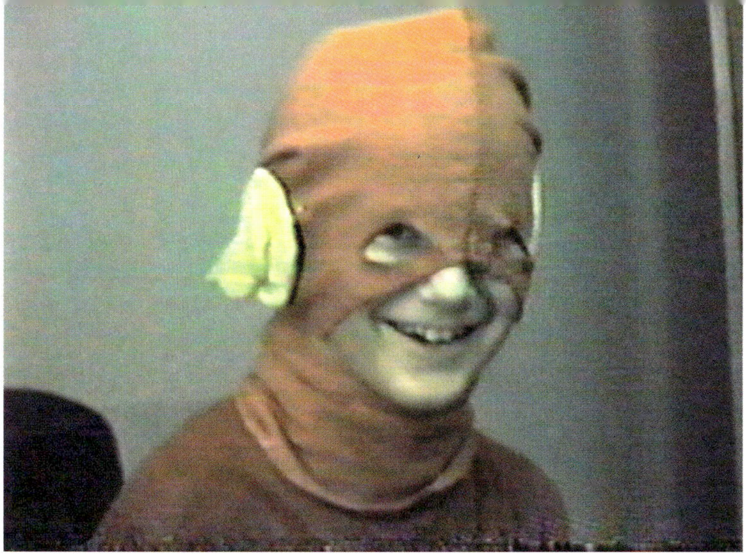

HOME MOVIES

From the day Dad brought home his first "portable" VHS video camera in 1984—a state-of-the-art, two-piece unit that easily weighed over twenty pounds—making movies became central to our adventures. Countless movies were written and directed, with the actors coming from an abundance of willing siblings and any neighbourhood kids lucky enough to be hanging around.

Making our own movies allowed us to kill bad guys and become wise guys, solve mysteries and save babies. We hunted Sasquatch and became superheroes. And of course, we did all our own stunts. We jumped off everything we could: fences, trees, roofs, schools, cliffs, and moving cars. As our movies improved, they went from being shown in the living room to the town hall, to being screened in independent theatres around the world on the film festival circuit.

Above: Aaron in a homemade Halloween costume. Uxbridge, ON. 1990.

Opposite: Stephen on the arm-powered bike as Benny mounts the Nizo Super 8 camera while filming for "Ski Boys." Uxbridge, ON. 2006.

Previous spread: On the set of Benny's second feature film, "Minor Setback," with Benny behind the camera, Matt Ottenhof on lights, and Dave Barber behind the wheel. Uxbridge, ON. 2000.

Clockwise from top left: Benny envisioning the Winking Circle video zine on cue cards pinned to his bedroom wall. Video editing station with Premiere Pro 1.0. David with a Winking Circle VHS tape. SOSA (Southern Ontario Sasquatch Association) film shoot. Benny looking through a broken TV set. The bloodied cast and crew from "Minor Setback" (from left to right): Dan, Mark Vanderwal, Aaron, Matt Ottenhof, Spencer Butt. Benny with Matt Capotosto and crew filming Andy McIlwride on the roof of an abandoned house, Uxbridge, ON, Early 2000s.

2003
2004
WINKING CIRCLE
2006
2005

After high school, we instigated a community film project that grew even larger, with more people, handmade costumes, many different set pieces, and subdivision homes fully transformed into visionary environments. These experiences were revelatory as we discovered the power of community filmmaking to bring a wide variety of people together and encourage them to use their innate creative skills. Making a film together became a powerful tool to positively impact our community.

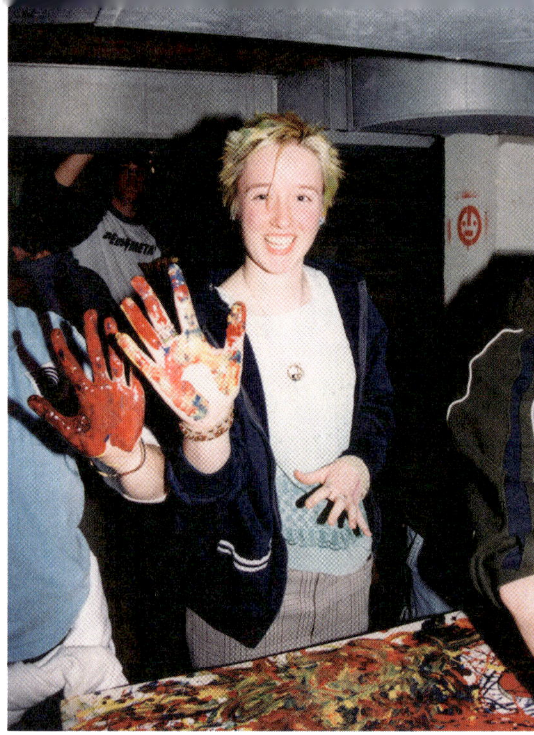

For us, the camera was a tool to experience life more deeply, to make connections with people, to get other people involved, to go on adventures, to transform our town.

Inspired by a tall bike and chopper bike zine called C.H.U.N.K.. 666 that we ordered by mail from Portland, Oregon, a few of us pitched in to get a welder. We organized our tools and taught ourselves to weld. We collected old bicycles, cut them up, and began creating art bikes. Soon, a fleet of hand-painted chopper bikes, spark bikes, butterfly bikes, tall bikes, and all sorts of rolling joy machines were cruising the streets of our sleepy little town. The once all-powerful TV set was dragged by its cord behind our art bikes, and the sparks ignited a fire of eccentric self-expression that was simply too powerful and hilarious to stop. Ridiculous times demanded ridiculous measures.

We called this group The Winking Circle. The name came from our logo—a twist on the world's most recognizable graphic symbol, the smiling face—except ours had a crooked smile with a winking eye. It was a playful symbol of positive public mischief.

This page (from left to right): Richard Barber, friend, Jon Perrott, Syd Healey, Sterling Healey, Rashmi Baird, Nathan Enkel, Ted Webb, Chris Clements, friend, Dan Evans. Critical Mass, Toronto, ON. 2001.

Opposite page (from top): Esther Knight at the first Winking Circle meeting. Winking Circle logo. 2000. Ted Webb, working on an early Winking Circle art bike. Uxbridge, ON. 2001. Photo by Claire DeAth.

Wink House. Uxbridge, ON. 2003.

WORK WITH WHAT YOU HAVE

Stephen modified Dad's Pontiac Bonneville into a field car using an oil tank for a bumper. Marsh Hill, ON. 2012.

We built all our early tall bikes out of old, discarded bicycles. It was empowering to build something so fantastic out of garbage—it challenged the idea that the best stuff was new. Instead of being consumers of mass-produced, store-bought products, we began to customize what we already had around. We transformed our old cars into art cars, screen-printed on used clothing, and built skateboard ramps out of scrap wood. It was much more rewarding to take what others had thrown away and transform it into something extraordinary.

Build a new relationship with material things. Don't be too precious about your stuff. Be open to personalizing it. Using it. Breaking it. Put a handprint on your jacket. Make your own logo for your clothes. Paint over the logos that are already there. Add a pattern. Do something to make it yours. Like Hundertwasser says: kick it. Put a dent in it. See yourself as an individual. What do the things around you say about who you are?

Top: Do you ever feel like your bike is a doorway to another world? Benny rides Dorothy. Vancouver, BC. 2018.

Bottom: Benny testing an early prototype of the "Blue Angel," the world's first tall bike flamethrower attachment. Vancouver, BC. 2016.

Top: If you can't go tall, go wide. A beautiful three-wheeler by Christian. Uxbridge, ON. 2008.

Bottom: Designed by Sarah Holtby, painted by friends and family. Willy's art van, driven across Canada for the Eccentrification Tour. Vancouver, BC. 2011.

BAD ART CLUB

It wasn't long before a fire of eccentric self-expression burned bright in our small town. We began to travel to the nearest city to take part in Critical Mass bicycle rides. We continued to host weekly meet-ups in our basement workshop, which quickly spilled out into the backyard. We sat around the fire, sharing our dreams, and then devised a screenplay as a way to weave all our wild visions together. We set out to be our own heroes by living an adventure rather than watching one.

Our BMX dirt jumps grew to fill an entire lot, and our barn ramps rivalled the skateparks we had only seen in magazines at the time. The energy was high and we wanted to permanently transform our town, so we began working with our town council to petition for a public skatepark. We hosted numerous events, raised all the money, then constructed our dream ramp—the "Tsunami Ramp"—for all to enjoy. All the while, everything was being filmed and compiled for a documentary that was to spread the message around the globe.

This Spread: The Winking Circle art bike gang eccentrifying the neighbourhood. Toronto, ON. 2003.

Previous Spread: In the summer of 2003, Winkers cut up over 2000 pop cans to decorate a house for a community film project in Uxbridge, ON.

Over time, The Winking Circle learned that when you stand against conformity, apathy, and consumerism, the world fights back. The first barn ramps were burned to the ground by local miscreants; the second barn ramps were constantly vandalized. The Tsunami dream ramp was, without warning or justification, sawn in half and moved out of town to a secret location to rot. As some of the Winkers grew up, the daily onslaught of consumer culture began to numb them into apathy. The Winking Circle was being assaulted from all sides, but a new phase was about to begin.

Above: Jantina behind the wheel of the Wink Van. Uxbridge, ON. 2003.

Right: Spread from the Winking Circle Zine. 2001.

Opposite page: Wink Van in front of Wink House during the filming of the Winking Circle Video Zine. Uxbridge, ON. 2003.

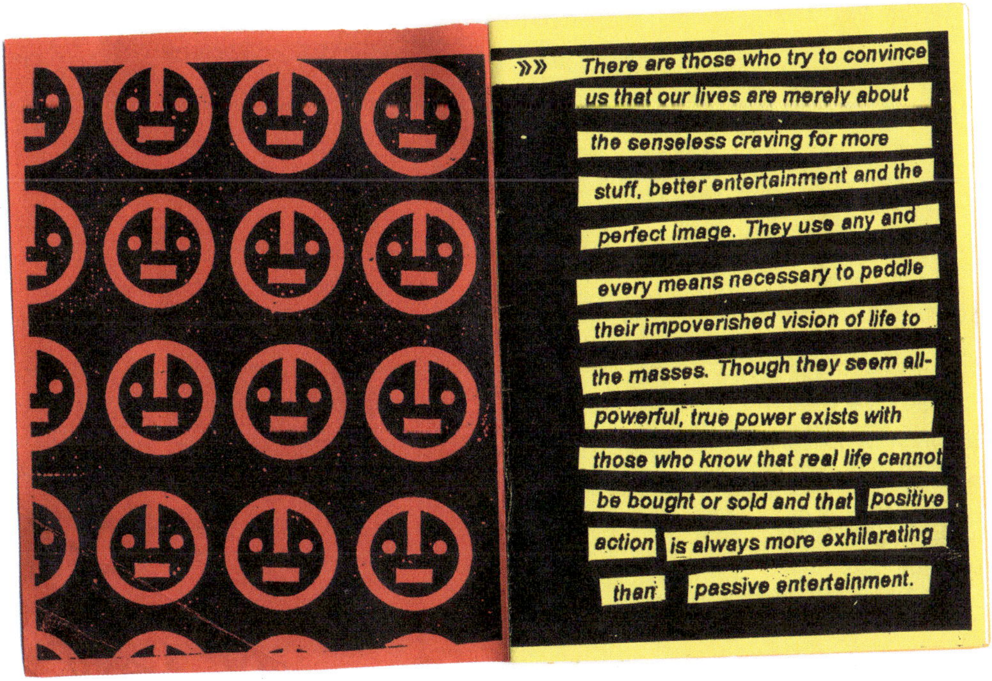
There are those who try to convince
us that our lives are merely about
the senseless craving for more
stuff, better entertainment and the
perfect image. They use any and
every means necessary to peddle
their impoverished vision of life to
the masses. Though they seem all-
powerful, true power exists with
those who know that real life cannot
be bought or sold and that positive
action is always more exhilarating
than passive entertainment.

Over the years, every meeting, event, adventure and act of joyful creative rebellion had been captured on film and video. Now was the time to put it all together. After labouring over hundreds of hours of footage, editing and reediting for months, the perfect cut was created: The Winking Circle Video Zine. A documentary of the beginning of The Winking Circle, an audio-visual celebration of everything the Three Beans stand for. A premiere was organized, the movie was shown in film festivals and shared in living rooms across North America. The audience wasn't large, but the response was overwhelming.

Opposite page: Benny films the tall bike gang with his Bauer S 715 XL Super 8 camera while Willy keeps the trike steady. Toronto, ON. 2003.

Above: The Winking Circle at Critical Mass in Toronto (from left to right): Caitlin Wood, Reva Carmichael, Willy Zenga, Dan Zenga, Melissa Russel, Eric Wood, Matt Ottenhof, Christian Zenga, Jonathan Perrot, Benny Zenga, Tim Jensen, Stephen Zenga, Aaron Zenga, Tedd Webb, Josh Veens. Toronto, ON. 2003.

"Let's make a movie" was a great rallying cry, but it was really just a ruse—a scheme to rally the troops, build the props, pull off the stunts, make some crazy contraptions, and test them out. Watching the movie afterward was a fun little bonus, but it was never the point.

Everyone who sees The Winking Circle Video Zine is impacted in their own way. Kids have been known to shut off the TV immediately after watching it to draw or build bike jumps. Jaded TV executives have been moved to tears, and people have made their own Winking Circle t-shirts. It has been a springboard for people to remember old dreams and envision new ones.

Above and Opposite: Winking Circle group photos at Willy and Dawna's place, The original Winking Circle meeting spot. Uxbridge, ON. 2001.

TRANSFORM EVERYDAY LIFE

When you set out to Transform Everyday Life, every day is a new opportunity to bring beauty to the world around you. Don't get stuck in the mundane; every moment can be filled with wonder.

Everything is sacred if you look at it properly.

From how you engage with your family and friends to your job or community, there are endless opportunities to transform the world around you. To transform everyday life is to bring a more beautiful, exalted essence into whatever you are doing. When you approach the way you dress, decorate your home, or prepare meals as a spiritual act of service, you bring more creativity and care to those actions.

Above: The Ramper Camper provides everything you need to live comfortably on the road: an extremely capable overland vehicle, a cozy place to sleep, and multi-configuration ramps to skate. What more could you want? Andy Anderson has found his happy place. Vancouver, BC. 2023. Photo by Gordon Nicholas.

Opposite page: The Ramper Camper transforms the sidewalk into a skatepark. Andy Anderson airwalks over ramp configuration #1: the box ramp. Vancouver, BC. 2023. Photo by Gordon Nicholas.

Previous spread: There's a lot going on in this photo and it captures most of the Zenga Bros' greatest loves: jumping BMX bikes, custom-built ramps, tall bikes, and filmmaking. Aaron on the Recumbent Ramp, Dave launching, Skinny Tim piloting the Cargo Tall, and Benny capturing it all on his Bolex 16mm camera. Vancouver, BC. 2016. Photo by Gordon Nicholas.

swatch

Electric micro house truck becomes a multi-configuration skateboard ramp. The Ramper Camper is complete with a wood stove, a bookshelf grind ledge, and a canopy which transforms into a box jump, wall ride, or mini ramp.

When he's not gleaming the cube, he's riding the razor's edge. Andy Anderson risks everything on a perilous frontside grind as Benny and Christian hold up their end of the bargain. Vancouver, BC. 2024. Photo by Gordon Nicholas.

An engineering masterpiece: The Joy Machine. A cargo bike that transforms into a touring tall bike that can be completely disassembled and fit in a travel box. Built for adventure, designed for joy.

Opposite: Often when riding tall bikes we get asked, “How do you get off that thing?” Willy, exploring New Orleans, thinking to himself, “Why would I ever want to get off this thing?” New Orleans, LA. 2018.

As you work toward creating your dream world, don’t forget to focus on all the ways you can positively impact the present moment. Moving through life with a sense of gratitude, joy and wonder will bring light to any situation you find yourself in.

Transform the world as you move through the world.

Above: Andy Anderson boosts an ollie off a boardroom table turned pyramid ramp, built as a set of furniture pieces designed to accommodate the urge to skateboard anytime, anywhere. These dream builds are sculptural, skateable objects — Prototypes for Play. Whether at home, in the office, or out on the street, any space is transformed by these multi-configuration rejuvenation stations. Vancouver, BC. 2024.

Right: Channeling the Z-Boys, Andy holds up a childhood woodworking project. Vancouver, BC. 2024. Photos by Gordon Nicholas.

Above: 50 50 grind on the Lamp Ramp, a six-foot-tall floor lamp consisting of an arched steel stand and an oversized steel lamp shade. Upon pulling a release pin, the counterweights can be removed, the arched stand tilts forward, and the lamp lowers to the floor, becoming a volcano ramp and rainbow rail.

Right: Andy getting his required screen time in on the desk ramp. With the pull of a lever, the desk is released from its standing position, slides down a hidden track and out onto the floor, transforming into a quarter pipe.

All these ramps were built for the critically acclaimed "Skate Break" video project, presented by Swatch and part of an art show at Trapp Projects. Vancouver, BC. 2024.

TAX
Matinée
MENS
GREAT
DO NOT

STATE OF THE ARTS
CULT
What's in store

THE ECCENTRIFICATION

Previous spread: In awe at the sheer creative grandeur of Ken Gerberick's studio. Ken was a much beloved and prolific assemblage artist and art car builder in Vancouver. Filming during the Eccentrification Tour. From left—Ken Gerberick, Benny and Aaron. Vancouver, BC. 2011.

Top: Christian supervises Benny as he lays out designs on Stephen's van in preparation for the Eccentrification Tour.

TOUR

The Zenga family began in 1971 with our parents' honeymoon road trip across Canada in a 1960 Chevrolet panel van. For our parents' fortieth wedding anniversary, we devised a plan for the entire family to get together and travel in a caravan to share community and creativity—and the Zenga Family Eccentrification Tour was born. Seventeen of us piled into two brightly coloured, hand-painted vans, and a couple of us rode our old motorbikes. We piled art bikes on the roof of one van and pulled the rest in a trailer behind the other.

Above: Stephen's van crosses the Burrard St. Bridge on its maiden voyage. Vancouver, BC. 2011.

We invested a ton of time and energy into hand-painting the full-sized vans, turning them into wildly colourful, eccentric art vans. We built a fleet of art bikes, because for a few of the days we planned to do a bicycle tour together—everyone from Dad and Mom, who were around sixty years of age, right down to Willy's youngest, who was six at the time. We were all in. Along the way, we did creative workshops and film screenings in small towns and different communities. Beyond just us doing a trip together, we wanted to have some sort of focus—it had to be bigger than just ourselves.

100

When we finally arrived in Portland, we ended up at the home of 'Megalon 5', C.H.U.N.K 666 member and the author of the zine we had ordered over ten years before. To our surprise, he wasn't the least bit chunky and if he did worship Satan he kept it pretty low key. He was incredibly hospitable, allowing seventeen strangers to take over his home and yard for a couple of days. When we left, he gave us the complete collection of C.H.U.N.K. 666 zines and we thanked him profusely for his crucial role in ruining our lives for the ordinary.

Opposite: Christian looks up from his sleeping bag while backyard camping 15 feet from a busy railroad track. Portland, OR. 2011.

Above: Willy's and Stephen's eccentrified vans fully loaded with a menagerie of tall bikes and other joy machines.

Right: Karl Anderson's amphibious tall bike. Portland, OR. 2011.

A highlight of the Eccentrification Tour was a ten-hour tall bike journey out of Vancouver to a remote campground in the mountains. Riding with family members ranging from six to sixty-four years old, out of the city, through subdivisions, past farmers' fields, up and down dark, winding hills into the night was an indelibly memorable experience. To travel on brightly coloured tall bikes in such a large group created a scene that those who witnessed it will not soon forget. The smiles, waves, curious looks and spontaneous cheers of pedestrians and fellow cyclists reminded us that our journey was not just for ourselves but, because of our tall bikes, a joyful experience we could share with others.

Above: Exploring the wild forests surrounding Rolley Lake Provincial Park, BC. 2011.

Opposite: Official tour mechanic Stephen keeping old vehicles running like new. Somewhere down the West Coast on the Eccentrification Tour. 2011.

Vans overheated, bicycles needed repairing, audio-visual equipment malfunctioned and went missing. Some of us got sick, others got injured, and everyone pissed somebody else off at one time or another. We cooked meals together, ate together, set up and tore down camp together. At the end of most days, we sat around campfires playing music, reflecting on the day, and laughing harder than we've ever laughed before.

On the last night of the trip we rolled back into Vancouver around midnight. We parked vans beside the grand old house that used to be the home of a couple of dozen Catholic nuns. We had been given permission to camp out in the backyard during our tour. To unwind we quietly made our way into the basement and sat in a circle of mismatched chairs, surrounded by books and pamphlets from the AA group that met there weekly. For the next couple of hours we reflected on our epic adventure. It had been forty years since the Zenga family was started by two idealistic, adventurous lovers, and it was incredibly fulfilling to continue the journey together.

WORK WITH WHAT YOU HAVE TO TRANSFORM EVERYDAY LIFE

Christian's riverside studio while studying for his Master of Architecture.

BE A FOOL

Above: Uxbridge legend Matt Ottenhof with a massive leaf bag jump for “Minor Setback,” our second feature-length film. Uxbridge, ON. 1998.

Right: Christian frames himself within a tattered billboard somewhere in Ethiopia, en route to South Africa by bicycle, while filming “Where Are You Go.” 2008.

Previous spread (left): Some people dream of planting a flag on Mount Everest. We have different dreams. Abandoned industrial pilings become a Sanctuary Space for David. Belcarra, BC. 2016.

Previous spread (right): Benny and David ride the double-decker tall bike in downtown Vancouver, 2016. To me, this image, captured by David, is a masterpiece. He shot it using a Fujica GS645W medium format camera on Ilford HP5 Plus film, which he processed himself. The fact that David managed to nail the timing, focus, and composition while riding the double-decker, which we built together, speaks volumes to me. –Benny

There are no guarantees when living the Way of Infinite Creativity. To Be a Fool is to be fully committed. Embracing your individuality, accepting your imperfections, and expressing your personal creative vision is what it means to Be a Fool.

It's human nature to want to fit in, but in a culture where fitting in tends to mean the mindless consumption of products and steady drip of entertainment, it's better to be laughed at as a fool than to fall in line as a follower. Now it's more important than ever to step out and discover your true self.

We need to become comfortable within the unknown.

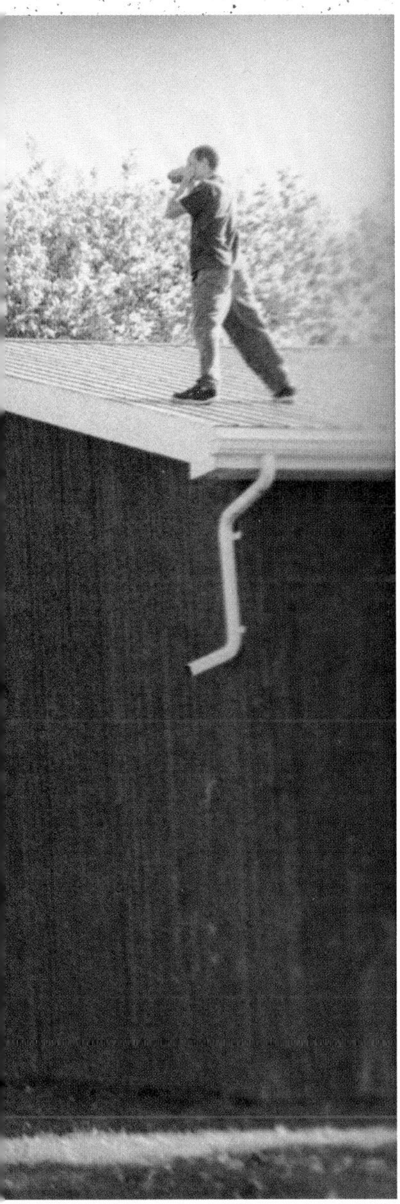

Foolishness is the precursor to transformation. Nothing new would be discovered without the fool. Inventors and geniuses, spiritual radicals and visionary entrepreneurs are always looked upon as fools at the beginning of their journeys. The fool is one who is willing to risk ridicule, scorn and rejection to follow their own path.

The fool has played an essential role in many religions, spiritual traditions, and Indigenous cultures throughout the centuries. Whether it's the medieval jester, the Zen trickster, or the Russian holy fool, the fool is uniquely able to challenge the ruling authority and question the norms of the dominant society. The fool lives beyond the accepted values of wealth, beauty, conformity, convenience, and power of our modern culture. Even today, if we are willing, we too can experience the joy and freedom of discovering liberating new ways to play the role of the fool in our world.

The fool specializes in magic, play and radical innocence.

In a world of extreme polarization and the temptation to harshly judge the Other, the fool refuses to take themselves too seriously. We must be willing to laugh at ourselves and remain open-minded, spontaneous and, above all, humble. Playfulness, authenticity and spontaneity allow us to continually see the world around us with fresh eyes and make connections with all people.

This page: Willy Zenga. Portrait by Gordon Nicholas.

Opposite: Willy hydroplaning at Floyd Bennet Field, an old military airport on the southeast side of Brooklyn. It is now the only legal campground in New York City. We set up camp there for a few nights to conduct our Apocalypse Bike Tests (ABT). We're still working out whether this is an effective flood bike or a lightning rod.

55
KODAK PORTRA 400
12

54
KODAK PORTRA 400

JOY MACHINES

The bicycle is the ultimate overland vehicle. It is an affordable, human-powered machine of precision and balance, which allows millions of riders around the globe to propel themselves forward in countless ways. But there is one type of bicycle that remains on the fringes. One that is only embraced by the daring, the creative, the foolish: the Tall Bike.

A tall bike is most commonly built out of two or more old bicycles stacked on top of each other and may also incorporate other pieces of scrap metal into its construction. Like the name implies, it is built to be taller than the average bicycle and can vary anywhere from five to twenty-five feet tall, limited only by your imagination and courage. Because it is constructed from discarded old bikes, scrap metal, and whatever else its creator may find, the tall bike symbolizes the revolutionary truth that trash can be transformed into treasure.

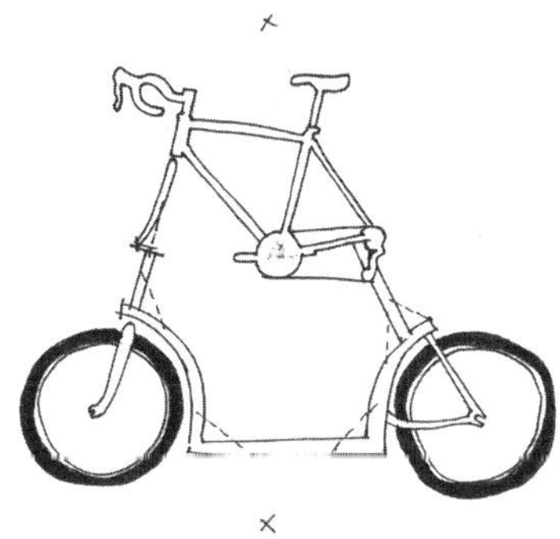

A tall bike is the perfect combination of the foolish and the functional, the ridiculous and the rational. To build a tall bike you must exercise your imagination, test your scrounging skills, practice your DIY initiative and ability to work with your hands. To learn to ride a tall bike you must have patience, courage, and a healthy sense of humour.

It gives you a break from the seriousness of day-to-day life and allows you to be foolish. We named our tall bike the Joy Machine because that's exactly how it makes you feel when you get on it—whether it's through the surprised reactions of people you meet, or simply cruising along up high. It's joyful, invigorating, and it makes you feel good. It reminds me of Steve Martin saying you can't play a sad song on a banjo. You can't be depressed on a tall bike.

Previous spread: Aaron leads the pack on the BMX tall, Willy follows close behind on "Riki-Oh," and Christian screams in terror, realizing his head tube is jammed, as he hurtles towards a very deep loading dock pit. East Vancouver, BC. 2012.

Opposite: Benny and David with "Daddy Longlegs" and "Mommy Longlegs" touring tall bikes, built using 1970's CCM tandem frames for the undercarriage. 2015.

116

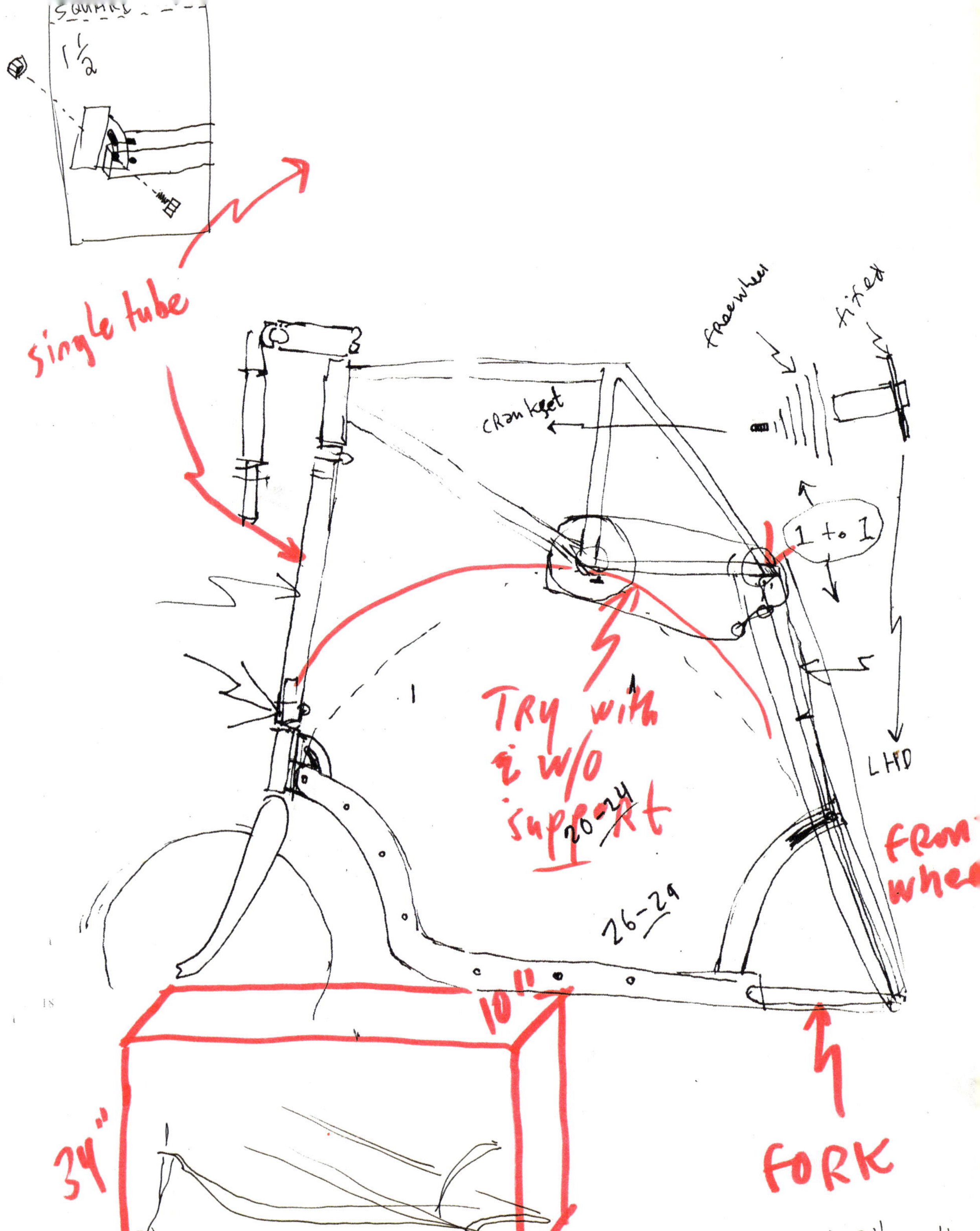

Tall Horse → 57" wheelbas

52" Wheelbase

Opposite: David and Owen racing in East Vancouver, 2016.

Clockwise from top: Benny jumps the Mini Tall that was designed to fit in a briefcase off a curb cut in NYC, 2006. The Lightning Bolt tall bike with a spare fold-up bike. The Joy Machine transforms from compact tandem, to mid-tall, to full-tall. Aaron with the Lightning Bolt frame set ready for paint. Aldergrove, BC. 2018.

Previous page: David rides his tall bike loaded up with camera gear and two skateboards. Stanley Park, Vancouver, BC. 2016.

Riding a tall bike is not merely about self-expression or attention-seeking; it's a vehicle of radical creativity. You transform any environment you pass through.

You make spontaneous connections, shocking the passerby, awaking them from their daily routine. Awakening them to a world where true joy and wonder cannot be bought or sold, but must be created and experienced.

This world is available to anyone with a willingness to use their imagination and actively put in motion their visions and dreams.

Left: Christian rides the H-Bike, built by Tedd Webb out of a discarded bed frame. Toronto, ON. 2004.

Right: Benny test rides the Tall Tall at the farm in Uxbridge, ON, before taking it to the city. 2007.

Seconds after my mom snapped this photo, I lost all forward rolling momentum then proceeded to answer everyone's favourite question: "How do you get down?" Naturally, I reacted with ninja-like reflexes, attempting to jump to the grass below—except my t-shirt got caught on the handlebars. What happened next was a grisly scene I dread will be released from my subconscious one day. All I know is that I ended up in a heap on the grass, the wind knocked outta me, with a 12-inch gash across my chest. Somehow, I managed to roll just in time to avoid the bike as it came crashing down next to me. I remember feeling badly for my mom, that she had to witness such carnage. To avoid writhing in agony in front of her, I struggled to my feet, walked it off, then choked out a laugh that I was fine. So yeah, that's how I got down.

Above: Were our designs maturing? Or were we descending further into madness? Dr. Viktor Zenga ready for lightning to strike.

Opposite: David, fully prepared for whatever may come, readies himself for an imminent escape from civilization. Somewhere in British Columbia, Canada. 2016.

This page: Sign painter from Dar es Salaam, Tanzania. 2008. Photo by Brian Vernor.

Opposite: Christian Zenga aboard the Tall Horse. Malawi. 2008. Photo by Brian Vernor.

While riding the Tall Horse, we discovered that the additional height of the tall bike, despite its added weight, somehow energized us beyond our normal limits. Whether it's through the laughter from strangers along the way, or some deeper wellspring of adrenaline we tapped into when riding at exaggerated heights, we found it nearly impossible to grow weary on the tall bike. Our 12,000 km journey from Cairo to Cape Town has proven this theory valid.

TALL HORSE

While documenting a four-month bicycle expedition across Africa from Cairo to Cape Town, we (Benny and Christian) brought another tall bike, the Tall Horse, to life. Using nuts and bolts, plumbing pipe, and angle iron that we found at the Merkato—Africa's largest market, located in Addis Ababa, Ethiopia—we stacked one bike frame on top of another to form a tall bike. Travelling by bicycle provided an immediate connection with the land and the local people. The Tall Horse transformed our encounters with the locals. It exaggerated our experience and reversed the dynamic of the spectacle.

We named it the Tall Horse, alluding to the giraffe, but also as a nod to the bike's roots as a "wheel horse." We hired a local artist to paint us a licence plate that said TALL HORSE, fixed it to the front, and started riding it every day.

Immediately, the tall bike completely transformed our experience. It transformed how local people responded to us. The attention shifted away from us as foreigners travelling through their towns and onto this insane, wild, hilarious bicycle. People pointed and laughed—it was an instant party. Entire villages. Literally a hundred people would flood the streets and chase us. We'd jump down, be surrounded, and let the bravest climb up and give it a ride.

Local bike mechanics would inspect it with a knowing eye, surveying the chain-line and construction. We'd converse in broken English, then fall back into the throng—lost in this crowd of people focused entirely on the tall bike. No one was paying attention to us anymore. It was all about this fun, wild bicycle.

People talk about the universal language of music. This was the universal language of play—and the bicycle is the perfect vehicle for that. The tall bike absolutely exaggerated that experience.

Top: Sign painter paints bicycle licence plate for the Tall Horse. Dar es Salaam, Tanzania. 2008. Photo by Brian Vernor.

Bottom: A monk captures hidden relics with Benny's camera on Kebran Gabriel Monastery Island, Lake Tana. 2008. Photo by Brian Vernor.

We learned countless lessons on that journey. While in Ethiopia, I visited a monastery on a remote island in Lake Tana. A monk was giving me a guided tour of the site, and I had my video camera trained on him, but his descriptions were rote and mechanical. When I paused to remove my shoes at the entrance to the chapel, the monk insisted on holding my camera. I passed it to him, then quickly decided to show him the basic camera functions and encouraged him to try it.

The monk resumed the tour, now operating the camera himself, and suddenly his voice came alive, full of warmth and engagement. He pulled back curtains and probed my camera into dusty cabinets, this time giving detailed descriptions of crosses, golden crowns, and a goatskin Bible from the fourteenth century, which he invited me to touch. He paused at a padlocked tomb and whispered that it contained the Ark of the Covenant.

The thing that moved me most that day was how the monk's energy shifted once he held my camera. Suddenly, he was actively contributing to how the story would unfold. Since then, I've made it a point to share cameras with my subjects so they can show me what they see.

Top: Benny Zenga rides the Tall Horse in Malawi. Behind him tobacco leaves hang to dry off a front porch. 2008. Photo by Brian Vernor.

Bottom: Local resident Stuate Chunga rides the Tall Horse in Champhira, Malawi. 2008. Photo by Brian Vernor.

Above: Boys pushing their homemade mountain cart in the Ethiopian highlands.

Our next expedition brought us to the Danakil Depression in Ethiopia—the hottest and most inhospitable place on the planet. The rocky ground resembles a barren, lunar landscape that is pockmarked by volcanic vents and covered in sulphur. When we were invited to film a bicycle trip across this hazardous region, we jumped at the chance, knowing that it would provide an opportunity to ride a tall bike where none had been before.

We worked for months leading up to the trip, fabricating a chrome-moly steel frame, which would be strong enough to survive the rugged terrain we would encounter. We designed the first ever touring tall bike that could be disassembled and reassembled in minutes. In most situations a tall bike is the element out of the ordinary. But in the surreal landscape of the Danakil, being on a tall bike felt like the only way to travel over this otherworldly landscape.

Top: Christian riding the Joy Machine within the heart of the Danakil Depression, one of the lowest and hottest places on the planet. Even though he sits atop a six-foot tall bike, he's still 400 ft below sea level. 2011.

Left: Benny and Christian walk towards Erta Ale, an active volcano, known locally as "the gateway to hell." Five years later, Werner Herzog followed in the footsteps of the Zenga Bros. while filming his documentary "Into the Inferno."

Following spread: During the expedition to the Danakil Depression a group of Toyotas sit in the sweltering Ethiopian desert, as their drivers search for a sliver of midday shade.

TOYOT
68715

21 REASONS WHY THE TALL BIKE IS THE ULTIMATE OVERLAND VEHICLE

1. Tall bikes are rolling works of art, interactive kinetic sculptures, creating a sense of wonder in an otherwise ordinary day.

2. Built with friends and human-powered, tall bike technology connects you with others and the natural world.

3. Tall bikes are DIY. You can't buy one; you have to build it yourself.

4. It's a rolling ladder. On a tall bike you can access places you wouldn't be able to reach otherwise: tree branches, fire escapes, and rooftops. You can hang posters and paint walls above the rest. You can see over fences and find empty pools.

5. On a tall bike you look down on cars.

6. Like skateboarding in the '80s and BMXing in the '90s, riding a tall bike is not cool.

7. Riding a tall bike is the coolest thing ever. You may laugh at yourself and make light of it, but inside you feel like royalty.

8. Escape the noise of the masses on a tall bike; whenever you ride, your head is in the clouds.

9. Riding a tall bike is difficult. Just getting up on it is a challenge. The greater the struggle, the greater the reward.

10. A tall bike is an exaggerated bicycle; all of the sensations of riding a regular bicycle are amplified.

11. A tall bike is the perfect tool to escape the blandscape.

12. The tall bike is an antidote to loneliness. A simple trip to the grocery store becomes an opportunity for delightful encounters filled with curiosity and laughter.

13. A tall bike tests your patience. When you ride a tall bike, you are forced to interact with people who have questions and ask "How do you get on that thing?" a hundred times a day.

14. Tall bikes are the ultimate post-consumer, pre-apocalyptic vehicle.

15. With the elegance of a sailboat and the strength of a pack horse, the tall bike is a ridiculously practical touring bike.

16. On a tall bike you are a modern-day explorer carrying your home, supplies, and tools everywhere you go, transforming any environment you pass through.

17. Little secret: On the path to enlightenment, an hour of sustained focus while riding a tall bike equals ten thousand hours of meditation in the Himalayas.

18. On a tall bike, you feel like a kid again. You get that amazing sensation of sitting on the seat with your feet not touching the ground.

19. Riding a tall bike is a natural high.

20. There is a deeper source of power available to us in life. You've probably heard stories of a mother lifting a car off her child, conjuring strength beyond her known limits; the tall bike taps into this mysterious power.

21. Tall bikes are fun. Simple as that.

Benny rides the Tall Tall on Queen West in Toronto. Photo by Martin Reis. 2007.

EXPERIMENT

To Experiment Boldly is to overcome the fear of the unfamiliar. It's about embracing a beginner's mindset and committing to trying new things, no matter how foolish you might look. Playing it safe and looking respectable is not an option for those engaged in audacious pursuits.

This page: David and Benny stake their claim for the next High Up Hut installation. False Creek, Vancouver, BC. Photo by Amy Walker. 2015.

Opposite page: False Creek High Up Hut. 2016.

BOLDLY

Constant, daring experimentation means nonstop action. It's the persistence of trying again and again, with scraped knees, bloody knuckles and aching muscles, to achieve what most think is impossible.

Only when you're willing to dedicate a ridiculous amount of time to mastering a skill others might see as useless, do you open the door to seeing your dreams and visions come to life.

Opposite: Overshadowed by greatness. Willy circles one of the greatest works of outsider art in the world, Watts Towers by Simon Rodia. Watts, Los Angeles. 2018.

13 METERS

HIGH UP HUTS

Like all kids, we loved tree houses, basement forts and secret hideouts. Lately, we have been experimenting with urban camping, graffiti living, and High Up Huts. We are interested in low-impact, artistic living in unusual and forgotten urban locations. We like to use salvaged materials to build whimsical structures that stand out against the cold backdrop of concrete, steel and glass that makes up so much of the urban environment. As adults, we're interested in forts as sanctuary spaces—quiet places that encourage contemplation.

It's important for us to design these places as something that is added to the environment or a place without damaging it. By utilizing the forgotten posts and pillars left behind by failed industrial projects, we put up a little lighthouse as a reminder to make a sanctuary space of your own—and of course to ease that kink in your neck. Look up. Tall bikes. High Up Huts. Anything to get people to look up from their phones.

After you build your sanctuary space, you don't own it. It's a gift to the city and anyone who has the courage to ascend its heights can kick back in your relax shack. If somebody destroys it, forgive them, because forgiving those who don't deserve it is called grace. And grace is what we need a lot more of in this world.

Opposite: Benny holds up a High Up Hut and ponders the truth of Friedensreich Hundertwasser's famous quote, "The straight line does not exist in nature." Vancouver, BC. 2016.

Right: Ricky-Oh parked outside of a secret hut built in the 1970s by a couple of high school boys, in the mountains somewhere near Stave Lake, BC. 2016.

Previous spread: You can complain about the modern urban blandscape or you can do something about it. False Creek High Up Hut. Vancouver, BC. 2016.

As skills are refined and deeper knowledge acquired, the designs get more intricate and the builds more audacious.
The mission doesn't change:
Build Dream Worlds.

Above left: Benny surveys the progress in between marathon fabrication sessions.

Above right: Whether building epic overland vehicles or forming the perfect curve, Alex is always grinding it out.

Right: When the project is this immense, sometimes all you can do is stare into the abyss. Willy and Christian focused on the task at hand.

All photos taken at Aaron's shop in Deroche, BC. 2021.

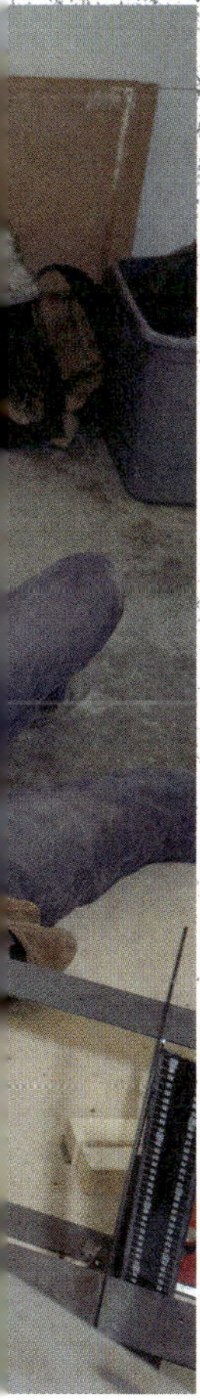

Top: The Secret Cove. An oasis of natural curves and lush foliage hidden in downtown Vancouver. Designed by Christian, built by the Zenga Bros. Vancouver, BC. 2021.

Bottom: For the modern roamers. Aaron's custom-built rolling home pulls a tiny office on wheels. Deroche, BC. 2021.

Above: Aaron and Christian hoist one of the many massive steel beams they fabricated by hand for the Tate Pavilion. Deroche, BC. 2020.

We started out building dream worlds for ourselves: forts, dirt jumps, barn ramps, skateparks, and High Up Huts. Now we design and build dream worlds to share with the wider world. As a kid, Christian spent countless hours creating his own personal spaces. Now he's designing immersive structures and environments for everyone to enjoy.

Right: Ike and Oly run through the angular shadows cast by the Tate Pavilion before the roof cladding was installed. Richmond, BC. 2022.

146

EXPRESS RECKLESS OPTIMISM

Previous spread: Owen leads the charge as Skinny Tim and the Zenga Bros. bomb down Burrard St. hill. From left to right — Skinny Tim, Aaron, Owen, David, Willy. Vancouver, BC. 2016.

This spread: With a portable studio strapped to the Cargo Tall, Benny and Emily are ready to conquer any mountain. Sunshine Coast, BC. 2019.

Without Reckless Optimism, the fool is powerless. Having faith in an outcome few can envision is what drives the fool to attempt the seemingly ridiculous. Ridiculous times demand ridiculous measures. The fool clings to the audacious belief that even the most hopeless situation can be redeemed. Believing in impossible dreams, the fool confounds the conformists and connects with fellow outsiders, misfits, and dreamers, to achieve the absurd.

Reckless optimism is not merely a positive feeling—it must be expressed in everything we do. It is expressed in the songs we sing, the celebrations we organize, the adventures we undertake, the clothes we wear, and the stories we share. Apathy leads us to believe that the world is beyond redemption and that our creative actions make no difference. Stepping out and ignoring the jeers and ridicule of the masses while creating dream worlds is the ultimate optimistic action.

Expressing Reckless Optimism is both the end and the beginning of the Way of Infinite Creativity. It continues the infinite loop that is the Wisdom of the Three Beans.

Without optimism we do not begin to create, and without creativity, optimism cannot endure.

Reckless optimism leads to relentless creativity.

Above: Inspired by Pakistani jingle trucks. Vancouver, BC. 2022.

Opposite: Is the tall bike a rolling sculpture or the ultimate overland vehicle? Maybe both. Emily testing the latest incarnation of the touring tall bike. Vancouver, BC. 2022.

POULTRY
&
EGGS

INFINITY CYCLE

We had relentlessly refined our tall bike designs, leading us to build the ultimate touring machine. A high-performance tall bike with an oversized undercarriage designed to haul more gear than a regular touring cyclist could ever hope to carry. We often carried not only our camping gear but all our camera equipment with us as well. This became an exhausting exercise. The only real problem with bicycle travel—tall or otherwise—is that it's human-powered...and humans get tired. And since e-bikes don't exist in our world, we had to get creative.

Right: Serious discussions about a nonsensical machine. Benny and Aaron, no strangers to the quixotic journey, put their heads together to solve the eternal question: "How can you ride forever?" Aldergrove, BC. 2018.

Opposite: The first day out on The Infinity Cycle. Aaron and Benny, the calm before the storm. Mission, BC. 2018.

Previous spread: I don't know what this is. At times I feel like I'm on a sailing voyage, on the upper deck with a hull full of supplies down below, schralping the streets. Such a strange, exciting synthesis of sensations. I love it. –Benny Zenga

We began to brainstorm about ways around this seemingly insurmountable problem: We came up with the idea of a double decker tall bike with a wrap-around undercarriage. This undercarriage would double as a sleeping platform. The tall bike would become more like a sailboat—where crew members could switch positions, allowing you to sail through the night.

Above: Benny climbs the ladder to Infinite Creativity while Aaron questions the decisions he's made in his life to get into this situation. Whatever your journey, The Infinity Cycle is the only way to get there. Mission, BC. 2018.

Opposite: Thor Heyerdahl would be proud. Navigating a modern day Kon Tiki through whatever nature throws at them. Fraser Valley, BC. 2018.

So, together with some of my brothers, we designed and built the world's first double-decker, vertical tandem touring tall bike: the Infinity Cycle. This groundbreaking joy machine allowed two riders to switch places without stopping, actually allowing us to ride forever—the dream of anyone who has ever ridden a bicycle.

After Benny got married and became a father of twin boys, he decided to upgrade the Infinity Cycle, modifying it so his whole family could ride it together—doubling its capacity from two riders to four. Where two riders could once ride forever, we were now able to ride it twice as long.

Infinity is just the start!

EXPERIMENT BOLDLY AS YOU EXPRESS RECKLESS OPTIMISM

BE A FOOL · CREATE EVERYWHERE · REDEEM EVERYTHING ·

THE FOOL'S CREED

CREATE EVERYWHERE

I am actively working every day to make this world a more beautiful place. My creativity is a manifestation of my love for this world. Every part of my life is touched by my creative impulse. I decorate, customize and transform everything I own.

MAKE WITH YOUR HANDS AS YOU BUILD DREAM WORLDS

REDEEM EVERYTHING

I am committed to making the most out of everything and every situation. As much as possible, I use recycled or redeemed materials. I believe that nothing is beyond redemption. I turn what others have discarded into something spectacular.

WORK WITH WHAT YOU HAVE AS YOU TRANSFORM EVERYDAY LIFE

BE A FOOL

I celebrate eccentric self-expression. I make myself vulnerable as I seek to love all unconditionally. Believing in impossible dreams, I ride on, confounding the conformists and connecting with the outsiders, misfits, dreamers, and achievers of the absurd.

EXPERIMENT BOLDLY AS YOU EXPRESS RECKLESS OPTIMISM

THE INVISIBLE PATH OF THE SECRET FOOL

The deeper one goes into the Way of Infinite Creativity the more one comes to see that the overwhelming beauty and intricacy of creative processes in the natural world are far superior to anything that the human mind can conceive or build. The desire to make things subsides and the desire to be a silent witness of the mystery of the Infinite within Nature becomes more prominent. One desires fewer and fewer material possessions and seeks to live as simply as possible in the most harmonious way possible with the natural rhythms of the earth. One recognizes that joy radiates from within and would rather be surrounded by Nature than human-made creations. One is satisfied with very small creative practices: poetry, wood carving, sketching, planting and gathering food, preparing meals, making the essentials for oneself.

The irony is that the more one becomes in touch with Infinite Creativity the less one feels the need to be constantly active. As one begins to see oneself united with the Infinite that is the Universe and everything in it, every act, no matter how small, becomes a creative act infused with meaning. The whole of life is a prayer of gratitude and wonder and the gift of consciousness with which we can behold the Mystery and Beauty of It All.

To Be a Fool is to free oneself from the unquenchable need to mindlessly fill one's life with things and experiences in the pursuit of happiness. It's to realize that you are a manifestation of the Joy of the Infinite, needing nothing beyond the realization of your Oneness with All, a childlike sense of wonder and a practice of radical gratitude.

Thank You, Thank You, Thank You. Thank You for Everything.

Owen, Aaron and Willy. Burrard Street, Vancouver, BC. 2017.

THE JOURNEY

We will continue this journey for the fellow creative fools we will meet along the way—for those who feel alone in this world, for those who see the world differently and suffer for it. For the ones who may have stopped creating long ago because they were told they couldn't draw well enough, sing in tune, or perform for the crowd. For those who were told that, in this world, some people are artists and some are not.

We are doing this for them. We are doing this for all of us.

Because we believe that there is no proper time and place for art. Art is for every day and everywhere. It is for here and now. Art is a way of living—it is the everyday expression of beauty, mystery and wonder. We believe that we were all born to make art, to wear art, to drive art, to be art.

We want to live in a world of Wild Creativity—a world where art, music, and self-expression are ever-present and celebrated. A world where front yards are filled with friends and families making music together and the outside walls of our homes are seen as canvases for artistic expression. A world where tall bikes roam every street, hand-painted cars roll down every highway, and clothing is colourful, eccentric, and meaningful. A world where art has no boundaries. A world where everyone remembers they are an artist.

Is this a foolish dream? Yes it is.

But we know we are not alone. We ride on, ignored by the masses, confounding the conformists, and making connections with the few who have held on for dear life to their most precious resource: Infinite Creativity.

Right now, more than ever, the world needs people who are willing to risk foolishness as they use their creativity to redeem the world.

The world needs you.

STREETS
STUFF
CREATE
EVERYWHERE
REDEEM
EVERYTHING
BE A FOOL
CREATE EVERYWHERE
REDEEM EVERYTHING
BE A FOOL
SUPER RICH
WAX
REDEEM EVERYTHING
BE A FOOL
CREATE EVERYWHERE
CREATE EVERYWHERE
REDEEM EVERYTHING
BE A FOOL

THE WORLD NEEDS YOU

GO INTO

FEAR

CALLING ALL WANDERING WEIRDOS, DAYDREAMERS, CREATIVE FOOLS, SKATE MONKS, TALL BIKE STYLITES, VISIONARY TENT DWELLERS, SECRET INVENTORS, FEARFUL POETS, SILENT SPOKEN WORD SCREAMERS, PEACEFUL PROTESTORS OF THE POLICE STATE, DISRUPTORS OF THE BLANDSCAPE, INSTIGATORS OF POSITIVE PUBLIC MISCHIEF, SECRET SKETCHERS OF VISIONARY UTOPIAS, DREAMERS OF INEXPRESSIBLE INWARD JOURNEYS, WISTFUL WAITERS FOR THE PERFECT TIME, BED-DWELLING SCREEN-SCROLLING FUTURE HOLY FOOLS, ZEN ARTISTS FOLLOWING INVISIBLE FOOTSTEPS, EXPLORERS OF WEIRD WORLDS, EXPRESSERS OF RECKLESS OPTIMISM, DIRTY FINGERNAILED, PAINT-STAINED, GRASS-STAINED, SCRAPED-KNEED CROOKED GRINNERS BUILDING NEW WORLDS IN FORGOTTEN SPACES.